BE
NOT
AFRAID

Living With Faith in the Midst of a Fearful World

Karen May

CONTENTS

$\mathcal{D}edication$

I dedicate this book to my husband.
He is my touchstone and my biggest fan.
I have been so blessed to have him by my side
as I have walked the incredible journey to this book.
He was there through my darkest fears, giving me
light and hope, and he is there in my brightest
moments helping me to bask in them.
I thank God for the gift that he has been to me.

PSALM 23

The Lord is my shepherd, I shall not want.
He makes me lie down in green pastures;
He leads me beside quiet waters.
He restores my soul;
He guides me in the paths of righteousness
For His name's sake.

Even though I walk through the valley of the shadow of death,
I fear no evil, for You are with me;
Your rod and your staff, they comfort me.
You prepare a table before me in the presence of my enemies;
You have anointed my head with oil;
My cup overflows.
Surely goodness and mercy will follow me all the days of my life,
And I will dwell in the house of the Lord forever.

When I read that the Bible says,
"Be not afraid" 365 times, I was curious.
First, to see if it was true—it's not, but Scripture
does say the phrase many times—and second,
to see what God tells us in each "be not afraid"
statement. Just as my fears have been many and
varied, I was sure that the moments that God tells
us not to be afraid would cover many areas.
Sure enough, I found this to be true.

It's easy to say "Be Not Afraid" from the comfort of a happy life, secure home, healthy family, and loving friends. Not so easy to say when looking down the edge of a cliff, standing in the emergency room, or the phone rings at two in the morning. Apparently, even standing in the presence of an angel is terrifying, otherwise they wouldn't start every appearance with some version of "Be Not Afraid." It's sort of like getting that call from the school nurse; you can hardly start listening until she says, "Everything is fine . . ." Be not afraid . . .

All of us experience fear. It is a normal response that helps us avoid danger and sometimes even pushes us into action. But there are times when it gets in our way, times when the fear prevents us from doing what we should and living as we could. We could let fear control our responses, but it doesn't have to be that way.

God tells us over and over that we are not to be afraid. He is not telling us to deny our feelings, but is rather telling us to recognize when they are appropriate and when they are not. He is telling us how to place ourselves with Him, knowing that He is always in control, if we will let Him be. God is teaching us to trust in Him, and to allow ourselves to be held by Him.

In this first volume, we will start at the most natural place: "In the beginning . . ." We will journey from the beginnings of a promise, all the way to the edge of the Promised Land. So, what exactly does God tell us not to fear? Let's find out.

HOW TO USE THIS STUDY

Start each lesson in prayer. Lay all your worries, anxieties, and cares in the strong and capable hands of your loving God. Ask for Him to open your heart to the lessons He has for you today, knowing that it is His love for you that draws you here. Know that He has called you out of fear and into peace. Lay down your burdens and come.

If you are doing this study on your own:
Remember to allow yourself to be in a place of imperfection. Be kind and forgiving of yourself. Allow God to work through the areas that are exposed in the lessons. Some of them will take time to work through. Let it happen, and be patient with yourself and with God.

If you are leading this study in a group setting:
This study is best suited to a small group setting. If you have a large group, it is recommended that you break up into smaller groups of six to ten for the discussion times. Group sessions are designed to last one hour. A sample schedule is as follows:

1. Share your responses to the homework from the previous week. Participants can share as much or as little as they would like. Leaders should try to help all participants have a chance to share if they would like. (10 minutes)

2. Read through each section aloud. When there are questions within the lesson, take a moment to allow participants time to reflect and write down their responses, then continue on with the lesson. These questions are for personal reflection and will not generally be shared with the group. After the Be Not Afraid section, spend a few minutes discussing any thoughts or questions from the lesson if needed. (20 minutes)

3. Have the participants read My Story and answer the Questions for Reflection on their own. Some of the questions may be difficult to answer. Encourage participants to give the answer that they have right now. None of our stories are complete, none of us are perfect, and some of our answers will help us see where we need to grow. That's a good thing. (10 minutes)

4. Discuss the Questions for Reflection as a group. This is not a time to solve one another's problems, or to heal one another's wounds, it is a time to process—and sometimes even to struggle—with what God has laid in front of us. It may take a few weeks or even months for someone to come to a comfortable resolution, and it is okay to let it happen. It is okay to leave something incomplete. God doesn't mind taking some extra time. (15 minutes)

5. Close in prayer – use the one in the book, or add your own. (5 minutes)

6. Personal Studies – Each week, we will have some homework to help participants see God's work in our lives throughout the week. Chances are quite good that participants will have many experiences each week that will bring our lesson to mind. It will just take a few moments, but is well worth your time.

Remember that these are sensitive areas in all of our lives. All things shared in this group are to be held with the utmost gentleness and confidentiality. This is holy ground, and should be treated as such.

However you are doing this study, go forward with courage, and *do not be afraid.*

Be Not Afraid
OF
DELAYS

How long would you wait for someone to fulfill a promise to you? A year? Two years? Ten? Can you imagine waiting twenty-five years for a promise from the deepest desires of your heart to be fulfilled? That is exactly how long it took for God to fulfill his promise that Abram would one day have an heir. After several years, what would you have done if you were Abram? Could you patiently wait on the Lord and His timing? Could you trust that you "heard Him" correctly for that long?

THEIR STORY

When Abram was seventy-five years old, God promised that he would become a father of nations and called him to go to a new land to settle and grow his family. Abram immediately left his home and settled in the land that God had promised, but years later he still had no descendants—no heir. One day God came to Abram in a vision telling him not to fear:

> *This word of the Lord came to Abram in a vision:*
> *"Fear not, Abram! I am your shield;*
> *I will make your reward very great."*
>
> –Genesis 15:1

Abram responds boldly, and from the heart, and immediately questions this supposed reward that he has already been waiting a long time to see.

> *But Abram said, "O Lord God, what good will your gifts be, if I keep on being childless and have as my heir the steward of my house, Eliezer?" Abram continued, "See, you have given me no offspring, and so one of my servants will be my heir."*
>
> –Genesis 15:2-3

God is not put off by Abram's question or his frustration, but instead takes him on directly, saying that his promise holds true, not through some technicality, but through Abram's own offspring. Then God takes it just one step further.

> *He took him outside and said, "Look up at the sky and count the stars, if you can. Just so," he added, "shall your descendants be." Abram put his faith in the Lord, who credited it to him as an act of righteousness.*
>
> –Genesis 15:5-6

Get the
Whole Story:
Genesis 12-15

It's a pretty incredible response to a valid question. How long will he have to wait for this promise to be fulfilled? God doesn't say, does He? He just reaffirms the blessing and says, "Wait for it. It's coming." Abram responds in faith and waits.

When something is taking a long time to come to fruition, what is your response?

Get anxious
Question

Do you bring your doubts and fears to God?

Yes

Do you sit quietly and give God an opportunity to respond and speak to your heart? What happens when you do?

- Sometimes I do sit - but many times I am moving on.
- I calm down

Sometimes, God's plans for us don't just seem delayed, but seem to be taken away completely. Later in Genesis, Isaac, Abram's promised son, has his own family and settles in the midst of the Philistines. However, the Philistines feel threatened by the great wealth that he has acquired and push him out of the land.

Each time Isaac finds a new place to settle, his servants dig a well. Once all the work is done, the Philistines come in and take over the land, pushing him out again. By the time Isaac has settled a third time and dug a third well, the Philistines finally back off. Shortly after, he has a vision.

> **The same night the Lord appeared to him [Isaac] and said: "I am the God of your father Abraham, you have no need to fear, since I am with you. I will bless you and multiply your descendants for the sake of my servant Abraham.**
>
> –Genesis 26:24

After this vision, the tables turn pretty drastically. The king of the Philistines arrives and offers peace.

> *Isaac asked them, "Why have you come to me, seeing that you hate me and have driven me away from you?" They answered: "We are convinced that the Lord is with you, so we propose that there be a sworn agreement between our two sides—between you and us. Let us make a pact with you."*
>
> –Genesis 26:28

Something changed in the Philistines; first kicking Isaac out and chasing him further and further away, then knowing that God was with him and feeling the need to make a pact. Was it the fact that he could find water everywhere he went? Was it that he never gave up? Was it that he didn't fight? It's not clear in the Bible, and it doesn't seem clear to Isaac either. All that is clear is that God reminded Isaac that He was with him, even in the midst of rejection. Moving was hard, and his challenges were real, but this was all part of God's plan.

Get the Whole Story:
Genesis 26

OUR STORY

It can be so hard to trust that God is working when it looks like nothing is going right. Each of us have our own responses to frustrating situations. However, in this story we can look at the events objectively and see the Philistines as instruments in the hand of God pushing Isaac toward the land God had chosen for him to settle all along.

How do you usually respond when things aren't working out the way you planned? Circle the words that apply:

Anger	Acceptance	Denial
Give up	Fight harder	Other: *frustration then acceptance*

Does this story change how you look at a situation that isn't going the way you think it should? Why or why not?

Abram and Isaac provide us with two examples of how we can react when things aren't going the way we think they we should be. Abram prayed—even complained—and then waited for an answer. Isaac didn't complain, but accepted the situation and moved on each time he was kicked out of his camp. Each time, God responded to them and renewed His promise to bless them and give them incredible numbers of descendants who would bring blessing to the world.

Through Abram, God tells us that we are to trust in what He has promised, even when it doesn't look like it will come to pass. It is okay to clarify. It is okay to ask. But then, we have to listen and wait for the answer. It may be that we have heard wrong and need a little more clarity, or it may be that we have to wait just a bit longer. Trust and know that God is faithful. He will fulfill His promises.

Isaac shows us that there are times when God says no, when He is blocking our path. It may be because we are supposed to go another way. It may be that the direction is right, but the location is wrong. Somehow, He will get in our way until we get it right. The challenge is to trust that He is working and be at peace with the redirection.

Be Not Afraid

What are Genesis 15:1 and
Genesis 26:24 telling us?

Be not afraid of delays and redirections in God's plan.

Trust in God and His plans for you.

MY STORY

Have you ever had one of those moments when you thought you heard a promise from God? Have you ever been asking and asking, and aren't quite sure how it is going to happen or if you should even hope anymore? I have.

My husband and I had two children and knew that we were ready for more. I could feel it in the deepest parts of my heart. There was one small problem. I had an undiagnosed abdominal problem that frequently flared up and knocked me out for the day with incredible pain shooting through my torso. There was no way that I could become pregnant and bear it.

I went to doctor after doctor to no avail, with no diagnosis or cure. Fine. Adoption is a wonderful way to give a loving home to a child who needed it, and my husband and I were both okay with going this direction. It was even one of those beautiful moments where my husband and I prayed together. In fact, it was the first time that we prayed together to ask God to guide our future. There was just one problem: We didn't hear the same thing.

As I prayed, I felt called to adopt through a private adoption. My husband, however, felt called to adopt from China. Neither of us felt peace in following the other one's plan. We would come together, pray, and have no resolution. Finally, we came together and wondered if this was really what God wanted for us. Had we even heard the calling right in the first place? God, what do you want from us? What good is the call if we can't do anything about it?

(continued)

Then, God came and spoke to us so clearly. As we looked at the adoption paperwork waiting to be filled out, my husband looked at me and asked, "Do you think that God wants us to have our own children?" As he finished that sentence, I could feel the peace of the Holy Spirit descend on both of us as we looked with astonishment at how clearly we felt that this was what God wanted. There was no division, no fear, no doubt. God had said, "Yes."

How could this be? I had been searching for two years for an answer to what was going on with my body, with no success. But this was so clear, that we both answered, "Yes." We threw away the paperwork that moment and I told God, "Okay. If that is what You have for us, then You better fix this body, because I just can't."

Three months later, my non-functional gall bladder had been diagnosed and removed, and I was pregnant. Never in my wildest dreams did I think it would be that fast and that easy. Never. Two children later, our family was complete. Just as God had promised.

QUESTIONS FOR REFLECTION:

1. Do you have an experience where your calling or your plan seem to be taking much longer then they should?

2. Have you turned to God in prayer about it? Have there been situations that helped move you forward, or has it been completely blocked with no signs of affirmation wherever you go?

3. If God is calling you to change directions, can you trust in these changes, knowing that the course adjustments are leading to something God has in store for you? Why or why not? How can you come to a place of trust?

4. If God is calling you to be patient and wait, can you do that after hearing these stories? What would help you wait?

 **CLOSING PRAYER:**

Lord, sometimes you lead us in mysterious ways. Sometimes the path is not very clear. We listen and we watch, and we hope that our feet are firmly on the path that you have laid before us. Help us to have faith and not be afraid of Your plan for our lives, even when it seems long delayed. Help us to hear Your voice as we ask for clarity, knowing that you are always near. Bless us, Lord. $Amen$

Week 1
PERSONAL STUDIES

Be Not Afraid

REST IN FAITH
and
LISTEN FOR ME

DAY 1

He took him outside and said, "Look up at the sky and count the stars, if you can. Just so," he added, "shall your descendants be." Abram put his faith in the Lord, who credited it to him as an act of righteousness.

–Genesis 15:5-6

This week, we are talking about how we can trust God's promises. The problem is that when God calls us to something, He doesn't always make it happen easily or even immediately. Sometimes, the message isn't even very clear. God's response to Abram in the verse above, however, seems to be very clear and affirming. Let's look a little closer and find out.

How many stars do you think Abram could see when God spoke to him in Genesis 15:5-6?

As we continue reading Genesis 15, we see that God asks Abram to make a sacrificial covenant to confirm this promise. Abram brings the animals, sets them up as required, waits, and the sun sets.

The sun sets.

Genesis 15:5-6 occurred in the middle of the day.

With that in mind, I'll ask again: How many stars do you think Abram could see when God spoke to him in Genesis 15:5-6?

Abram must have been confused as he stepped outside into the bright sunshine. There were no stars to count. He had no knowledge of the stars that were hidden behind the brightness of the sun. The only ones he would think of were the ones that were coming that night. They would start with a small star in the evening sky, and slowly grow in number until the sky was flooded with so many stars that they would be impossible to count. This was no message of immediate fulfillment, but a promise that his descendants were coming - starting small, but growing quickly to something beyond the ability of anyone to measure. It may not have been immediately clear, but Abram was being asked to trust and wait, and to enter into a covenant. This was a promise that would be kept, and Abram was able to see it.

1. How would you respond to a message like the one Abram received in
    Genesis 15:5-6?

2. Are you being asked to trust and wait in your life? How?

3. Does this story help you to wait? Why or why not?

For just as from the heavens the rain and snow come down and do not return there till they have watered the earth, making it fertile and fruitful, giving seed to him who sows, and bread to him who eats, so shall my word be that goes forth from my mouth; it shall not return to me void, but shall do my will, achieving the end for which I sent it.

–Isaiah 55:10-11

I love this verse. When I am going through a challenging time, I can come here and remember that even if I am getting it all wrong, God's work will be done. It's just a matter of whether or not I am going to help it or hinder it a little.

In the movie *Evan Almighty*, there is a moment when Evan's world has completely fallen apart. As his wife sits at a diner, miserable in their situation, God shows up as a waiter and reminds her of her prayer for her family to be closer as they moved to a new city. He says, "Let me ask you something. If someone prays for patience, you think God gives them patience? Or does he give them the opportunity to be patient? If he prayed for courage, does God give him courage, or does he give him opportunities to be courageous? If someone prayed for the family to be closer, do you think God zaps them with warm fuzzy feelings, or does he give them opportunities to love each other?"

This week, we are sitting with frustrating moments where we are waiting for God. We are looking at times when God's plan doesn't seem to be what we asked for. Fortunately, God's time is not the same as our time. We may not be ready for what God has for us, and we may not be hearing God's will for our lives very clearly.

Today, we will sit with the fact that all we have to do is be willing to cooperate. The rest is God's work anyway.

1. What do you think Isaiah 55:10-11 is saying to you right now?

2. Does that change how you are experiencing God's work in your life? How?

3. If God's will is going to be done anyway, what would be the benefit in participating in it?

DAY 3

Then the Lord said, "Go outside and stand on the mountain
before the Lord; the Lord will be passing by." A strong and heavy
wind was rending the mountains and crushing rocks before the
Lord—but the Lord was not in the wind. After the wind there
was an earthquake—but the Lord was not in the earthquake.
After the earthquake there was fire—but the Lord was not in
the fire. After the fire there was a tiny whispering sound.
When he heard this, Elijah hid his face in his cloak and went
and stood at the entrance of the cave.

–1 Kings 19:11-13a

My friends know that I have many God moments. Whether God speaks to me through prayer, or through a situation where it is clear that God is saying, "This is the path, walk in it" (Isaiah 30:21), they happen all the time. Because of this, I frequently have people complain to me that God doesn't speak to them, and they would really like to hear Him.

The funny thing is that each time someone complains to me that God doesn't speak to them, they almost immediately tell me about two or three times that they have felt God interact with them, or lead them to do something that they would not normally have done. Every time. They hear it, but they don't recognize or acknowledge that this could be God.

I think that we are all programmed to expect God to speak to us in a loud booming voice, or we hope to have some billboard with our name on it and our directions listed below. However, God is rarely so loud. Elijah experienced this as he waited for God to come in 1 Kings 19:11-13. God was not in the earthquake, wind, or fire, but was a small whisper.

Our lesson this week from Genesis 15 included one of those God moments for Abram. We might assume that these conversations with God were out in the open—a small man talking to booming voice coming from the sky—but, look a little closer. What if you read the story from the perspective of prayer? What if this is a small voice in Abraham's heart? What if this is a very personal message for him that no one else can witness? It is possible.

So for the rest of this week, our homework will be very simple. We're going to list some of those God moments each day. It won't take you long, but at some point in your day, or even at the end of every day, look back and see where God led you, where God spoke to you, and where God corrected you. Not every God moment occurs on the mountaintop with thunder and smoke, most of them occur in the valley, in our every day, in small, quiet whispers. Look for Him. Write it down. Remember.

Day 3

Day 4

Day 5

Day 6

Be Not Afraid
OF
OBSTACLES

People fly across the Atlantic Ocean every day. But in 1928, when Amelia Earhart did it, she was the first woman to fly across the Atlantic Ocean, and one of a select few who had ever been able to accomplish the feat at all. As she prepared for her historic flight, she had one mishap after another.

The plane left from New York, but had to stop in Canada because the weather was so bad. As they waited for the weather to clear, one of the pilots who would be flying with her got drunk each night and would be unprepared to fly in the event the weather cleared suddenly.

After days of anxiety and frustration, Amelia decided to lighten the load on the plane to enable it to fly in the icy weather that showed no signs of clearing. She took out all provisions, only keeping the amount of fuel need to get to their destination, and finally started her journey.

Even at the end, there were obstacles to overcome. They didn't have enough fuel to make it to their original destination of Paris; instead they landed in a field in South Wales. It didn't matter. None of the obstacles changed the result in the end. The flight was successful.

In our lesson today, we will walk with the Israelites from Egypt to the Promised Land. There were many obstacles in their way. There were many times of doubt and fear. Yet, through them all God was faithful, and their obstacles were overcome.

THEIR STORY

When the Israelites were freed from slavery in Egypt, it was a pretty amazing thing. After the tenth and final plague, the Egyptians not only freed the Israelites, but begged them to leave, giving them silver, gold, clothing, and anything else they asked for. It was a pretty good deal.

But, it wasn't long before Pharaoh's anger returned and he decided to pursue the Israelites and bring them back. The entire army was dispatched and caught up to the Israelites at the Red Sea. With the Red Sea in front of them and Pharaoh's forces behind them, the people were terrified. These were slaves, not soldiers. They had no way of fighting against a trained army.

> *In great fright they cried out to the Lord. And they complained to Moses, "Were there no burial places in Egypt that you had to bring us out here to die in the desert? Why did you do this to us? Why did you bring us out of Egypt? Did we not tell you this in Egypt, when we said, 'Leave us alone. Let us serve the Egyptians'? Far better for us to be slaves of the Egyptians than to die in the desert."*
>
> *-Genesis 14:10-12*

The obstacles loomed large, and it was easy to see that this was the end. God's miracles—from the plagues to their release from slavery—had been quickly forgotten:

> *But Moses answered the people, "Fear not!*
> *Stand your ground and you will see the victory the Lord*
> *will win for you today. These Egyptians whom you*
> *see today you will never see again. The Lord himself*
> *will fight for you; you have only to keep still."*
>
> –Exodus 14:13-14

Keep still. That's a pretty big request when you are facing an entire army. This seemingly insurmountable obstacle was really just a small interruption. In fact, God responds to Moses in the next verse saying, "Why are you crying out to me? Tell the Israelites to go forward." (Exodus 14:15). God doesn't even see that there is a reason to be worried. He's had their back from the beginning, and He isn't leaving now. All the Israelites have to do is watch as they are protected and delivered once again. Nothing has changed.

We know the rest of the story—the sea opens up, the Israelites cross on dry land, and Pharaoh's army is swept up as the sea returns to its normal state. Easy.

If you heard a call to stand still in front of an army coming for you, what would your reaction be?

Why do you think the Israelites stayed?

Get the
Whole Story:
Exodus 3 and 7-14

Of course, crossing the Red Sea is only the beginning of the journey. The Israelites still have to get to the Promised Land. As they wander through the desert, they pass through region after region, town after town. At one point, they ask permission to walk through the territory of Sihon, the king of the Amorites. It's an odd story. The Israelites promise not to take anything from fields or vineyards, nor water from any well. "We will go straight along the royal road until we have passed through your territory." (Numbers 21:22). Simple enough.

Sihon not only says no, but gathers his forces to attack the Israelites before they arrive. A bit of an overreaction. Now, instead of walking through without disturbing anything, the Israelites fight and defeat Sihon, taking over the land.

Moving on, they start towards Bashan. The king of Bashan, named Og, decides that Sihon had a good idea and marches towards the Israelites in a military attack. It had to be a little frightening from the Israelites' perspective, but God reminds them that He is still with them.

> *The Lord, however, said to Moses,*
> *"Do not be afraid of him; for into your hands I will*
> *deliver him with all his people and his land."*
>
> —Numbers 21:34

Once again, the Israelites defeat their enemy, Og, and take possession of his land. It becomes a pattern. These obstacles aren't quite as bad as they seem.

Get the
Whole Story:
Numbers 21:10-35

The final obstacle comes when the Israelites make it to the edge of the Promised Land. As they prepare to enter, Moses reminds them of their victories in the desert from Numbers 21.

> *"Your eyes have seen all that the Lord, your God,*
> *has done to both these kings; so, too, will the Lord do*
> *to all the kingdoms which you will encounter over there.*
> *Fear them not, for the Lord, your God, will fight for you."*
>
> –Deuteronomy 3:21-22

They wandered the desert for forty years, survived on manna, were given water from a rock, and saw miracle after miracle. As they face the powerful and intimidating people occupying the land they are to inhabit, they remember that any obstacle is God's to overcome. They can finally trust that if God is calling them to go to the Promised Land—even if it looks impossible—they can go.

Describe a time when you have felt called to something, but found that there were obstacles in your way.

Looking back now, can you see how you got through it? Can you see what gifts or assurances God gave you through that struggle?

OUR STORY

In times of struggle, tragedy, or anxiety, it is very natural to wonder or question if God is present in the situation. In the face of obstacles such as these, don't we all have our moments of doubt and uncertainty? The verse in Matthew where the disciples see Jesus after the resurrection always helps me feel better about my own doubts:

"When they saw him, they worshiped, but they doubted."

–Matthew 28:17

It is important to note that the Gospel ends only 3 verses later. The disciples have been with Jesus throughout his entire ministry, seen all the miracles, heard all the stories, and are standing in front of him after he has died, and risen again. And they doubt. Really?

The trick is to stand in our doubt, sit in our fear, and actually ask the question, "Where are You in this?" Then we must look for the answer, and sometimes we must wait. If we allow the Lord to lead us, then it is precisely in these moments that our incomplete faith (and it will be incomplete until we are standing in heaven) can be adjusted and made to be so much more full.

Be Not Afraid

What are Exodus 14:13-14, Numbers 21:34,
and Deuteronomy 3:21-22 telling us?

Be not afraid of obstacles.
Let God use them to
build your trust.

My daughter really wanted to go out of state for college. The problem was that with three younger siblings, paying double the cost of an in-state college was not in the plan.

As the two of us struggled with this obstacle, I asked some friends to pray for her. One of them asked if my daughter and I had been praying about it together. Well, no. This really wasn't something God needed to be bothered with anyway. I just needed them to pray that my daughter would quit arguing with me and find a reasonably priced college. Obviously, that was not the right answer.

My friend reminded me that God was the one who knew where she should be going in the first place, and we just needed to pray that *we* would know. From that moment, we started asking for clarity. I prayed, "Lord, you know where she belongs. You know which college will be the best for her. Open that door wide, and close all the others, so we will know, too."

Sure enough, she found a college that she knew was for her. It was out of state and very expensive, so we had to wait for the scholarship offers to come in. School after school sent the most pathetic financial packages. One even sent an apology with their offer, admitting that it really wasn't very much. Even her "safety" school didn't give her anything. Doors were closing left and right. And still, we waited.

Finally, the scholarship offer came from her dream school. My husband and I had given her a cost limit that she had to meet in order to go anywhere. The scholarship brought the cost of the school, plus the more expensive, faith-based dorm she wanted, to exactly what we required. Exactly. Door wide open.

Now, whenever we are discerning any direction, or facing any obstacle, this is our prayer: "Open the door we need, Lord. Close all the rest." ❧

QUESTIONS FOR REFLECTION:

1. *Do you have something that you think God doesn't need to handle, because you've "got it" right now? What is it?*

2. *What would you ask of God if you were to invite Him into the situation?*

3. *What are some experiences you have had that help you to trust that God will be there for you in this?*

4. *Some people keep a prayer journal, or even a list of their prayer requests on their phone or computer. If you kept a prayer journal, what would it look like when you reviewed it after a month?*

If you haven't done it before, try keeping track of your prayer requests for a while. Look back occasionally, and see which prayers have been answered and how.

CLOSING PRAYER:

Lord, we praise You for the obstacles in our lives. In them we discover our strength, our resolve, and our fortitude. We know that You can use all things for the good of those who love You. Give us courage as we face our challenges, and bless us in our perseverance. Bless us, Lord. Amen

Week 2
PERSONAL STUDIES

Be Not Afraid

REMEMBER
GOD'S
FAITHFULNESS

See, upon the palms of my hand I have written your name.

–Isaiah 49:16

This week, we looked at God's command to the Israelites to stand still and watch His saving work. Up until this point, they have had little experience with God's faithfulness, and it had to be hard for the Israelites to imagine that God thought they were worth saving. They needed to experience His faithfulness over and over again until they could believe that it was true.

It is hard for us to sit still and wait. It can be harder to sit still with God, seeing all that we are in His eyes. However, we are told over and over that we are precious, we are beloved. We are worth saving, and God is faithful. This week, we will sit with that. We have only to keep still.

1. *List three blessings that God has given you since the start of this study:*

2. *Do you believe that you are beloved by God? Why or why not?*

3. *With the understanding that you are beloved, this week, be looking for those moments of affirmation and love from God—your "angel kisses." Each day this week we will write about one of them. Be sure to pay attention.*

DAY 2

Rely on the mighty Lord; constantly seek his face.
Recall the wondrous deeds he has done, his signs and
his words of judgment.

–Psalm 105:4-5

This week, we discussed the wanderings of the Israelites from the Red Sea all the way to the Promised Land. It wasn't an easy path, and it was a pretty rough start. Let's look at a few of the times when God provided for the Israelites in just the first three months of their wandering, and see how the Israelites reacted. Look up each of these scriptures and answer the following questions for each:

a.   *What was the Israelites situation?*
b.   *What was their reaction to the situation?*
c.   *How did God provide?*

1.   *At the Red Sea: Look up Exodus 14:10-22*

   a.

   b.

   c.

2. *At Marah: Look up Exodus 15:22-25a*

   a.

   b.

   c.

3. *In the Wilderness: Look up Exodus 16:3-5*

   a.

   b.

   c.

4. *In the desert: Look up Exodus 17:1-5*

    a.

    b.

    c.

Every time the Israelites were afraid, God provided for them in spite of their fear. They complained and God answered them with comfort and blessing. Eventually, they were able to trust in God's faithfulness and enter into the Promised Land instead of being conquered by their fear.

It is important for us to remember what God has done for us, so that we can be confident that He is present with us even in the most fearful situations.

1. *Give a couple examples of prayers that have been answered or times that you believe God has intervened in your life.*

2. *If you are struggling with something right now, do these reminders help you have faith that God is present in this current situation? If you are not, do they help you have faith that God will be present when something does come?*

3. *Write today's "angel kiss" from the Day 1 assignment here, so you can add it to the moments you can remember.*

For God commands the angels to guard you in all your ways.

–Psalm 91:11

I was taking my daughter to lunch one afternoon, and I really needed a good parking spot. If I couldn't get one at the door, we probably wouldn't go to lunch, and she really needed to go to lunch. Most of the time, a lunch date doesn't have such weight to it, but this one was different. The week before, my daughter broke her arm badly enough to require surgery. She was having a hard time with the pain medications, and could hardly stand without support because of the dizziness they caused. She had been feeling terrible for days, hadn't returned to school or regular activities, and she just needed a moment of "normal." I wasn't going to be able to carry her, so a good parking spot was key.

Now, I have an angel I've named Parker that I call on occasionally when I need a good parking spot. It's kind of a family joke, but as we entered the crowded parking lot that day, I asked Parker to please get me that spot I needed, knowing that God could send an angel for something even as minor as this.

As we entered the parking lot, someone walking very, very slowly blocked my path as she walked across the road to get to her car. I couldn't believe how slow she was! But, given my experience with God, I waited and watched. Sure enough, as she cleared my path, a car ahead of me started to pull out of a parking spot—the one right in front of the door of our restaurant. Obstacle met, blessing received. My angel kiss for the day.

For the rest of this week, write down your own "angel kisses."

What was it? Why was it meaningful to you? What is it like going back and remembering it? What would be the value in keeping a list of "angel kisses" to be able refer to on occasion?

Day 3

Day 4

Day 5

Day 6

Be Not Afraid
OF
SUFFERING

It is often said that one of the marks of a saint is that they can find joy in their sufferings. It brings to mind old cliché stories of saints who were born praying, floated through life, and never struggled with suffering the way most people do. It is hard to imagine a normal person being joyful in suffering, but even today we can find examples of this wonderful gift.

Recently, my friend Mike was diagnosed with stage four prostate cancer. It's a scary diagnosis to begin with, and it would be understandable if Mike withdrew into himself to fight this battle. However, rather than feeling sorry for himself, he saw his illness as an opportunity to serve others as Christ would serve. One day as Mike was waiting for treatment, he thought to himself, "If Jesus were sitting here, He wouldn't be sitting in this chair, He'd be doing something," and started looking for what Jesus had for him to do. He began to speak with another patient waiting for their treatment, offering words of comfort, peace, and hope. He shared the experience of his diagnosis as a walk of faith— turning off the television, getting rid of all distractions, and walking with God through the whole thing. As the other patient was called back to start his therapy, another person in the waiting room said, "I couldn't help but overhear what you were saying. Can I talk to you?" As that person left, one person after another said the same thing, until finally an older gentleman told Mike that his words had been like a vitamin to his soul. He was a preacher who was struggling with his cancer diagnosis, looking for a sign of hope and peace, and Mike had given it to him. As this incredible group of people finished their treatments, Mike asked the preacher to lead them all in prayer. Just by asking Jesus to show him what to do in the midst of his suffering, Mike had changed the atmosphere of the entire room. Everyone there left in a very different spirit than the one they had when they entered.

Mike is a faith-filled man and spends time in prayer and study, but he's really not much different than you and I. He found a place of joy in the midst of his illness by acting as he thought Jesus would. He exudes joy, and it is contagious.

In this lesson, we will meet two women in Genesis who were told not to be afraid in their suffering. Through their stories, we see how we may find some of this joy for ourselves as we confront suffering in our own lives.

THEIR STORY

Hagar's story is a pretty juicy one. God still hadn't given Abram (who is now named Abraham) an offspring and Sarah, Abraham's wife, was well aware that time was not on her side. She takes matters into her own hands, telling Abraham to have a child with her servant, Hagar. This wasn't an uncommon practice at the time, as the child would be Abraham's legitimate offspring and an heir if Sarah never had a son.

Things were all well and good until Sarah actually got pregnant and had a son of her own. Her son Isaac would be now be the heir that Abraham was promised twenty-five years before, but there was a special place in Abraham's heart for his first son, Ishmael, and for his mother, Hagar. Not surprisingly there was a bit of tension in the camp and Sarah wanted none of Hagar's privileged attitude. It all came to a head, and Sarah demanded that Hagar should be expelled from the camp. God even affirmed the move telling Abraham to do as Sarah asked.

After being expelled, Hagar wandered aimlessly in the desert. She came to a place of desperation and despair, leaving her son to die as they ran out of water and had nowhere to go. It was at that moment God stepped in.

> *God heard the boy's cry, and God's messenger called to Hagar from heaven: "What is the matter, Hagar? Don't be afraid; God has heard the boy's cry in this plight of his."*
>
> –Genesis 21:17

At that moment, she was able to see what had been in front of her the whole time:

> *"Then God opened her eyes and she saw a well of water. She went and filled the skin with water, and then let the boy drink."*
>
> –Genesis 21:19

Hagar had given up at the very place where she was to be saved.

Get the Whole Story:
Genesis 16, 17, and 21

Briefly describe a time when you felt like things were hopeless and were ready to give up.

Looking back, was there a moment that things turned around for you? What happened?

In our next story, God's promise to Abraham of numerous descendants is becoming a reality. Abraham's grandson Jacob, also known as Israel, has two wives, two concubines, eleven sons, and one more on the way. These sons become the heads of the twelve tribes of Israel.

While Rachel is Jacob's second wife, she is actually his favorite; the one he has loved from the very beginning. On his first wedding day, Jacob thought he was marrying Rachel. Instead he was tricked into marrying Rachel's older sister, Leah, by his father-in-law. Jacob then works seven more years to earn the right to marry Rachel as well. (An entertaining story in its own right—check it out in Genesis 28-29).

In Biblical times, children, especially sons, were seen as a blessing from God, and infertility was an indication that you were not in God's favor. After being barren for many years and watching her sister and two servants provide ten sons for Jacob, Rachel finally had a son of her own. His name was Joseph.

At the point we enter her story today, Rachel is delivering her second child but the delivery is difficult, and she is at the point of death. Her midwife gives her these words of comfort:

> **When her [Rachel's] pangs were most severe,**
> **her midwife said to her, "Have no fear!**
> **This time, too, you have a son."**
>
> –Genesis 35:17

It seems like a strange thing to say to someone as they are dying. I'm not sure those are the words I would have chosen had I been the midwife. But, in this time period and culture, sons were very important, and Rachel dies knowing that God has blessed her. The family now has the foundation to become a nation. Each of the sons will be the head of a tribe that will be held as a lineage for all generations of Israelites to come. God's promises continue to be fulfilled.

Even so, "Have no fear!" seems to be a bit out of place here. She is dying after all. But, this is where we are reminded that for those who believe, death is not final. Death is not an ending, but a transition to the ultimate goal of each of our lives. As Paul says:

> *At present we see indistinctly, as in a mirror, but then face to face. At present, I know partially; then I shall know fully, as I am fully known.*
>
> –1 Corinthians 13:12

Death is not something to fear, but something that we are called to see within the context of a much greater reality.

For most of us blessings in death are difficult to see, because our vision is so clouded by loss. I think it is important here to understand that being unafraid does not mean being unemotional. Loss is loss, pain hurts, grief is real, and denying these things can cause real problems. However, our faith not only gives us hope for life beyond physical death but also gives us comfort that God is present and working even in this.

Get the
Whole Story:
Genesis 29:31-30:
24; 35:16-29

OUR STORY

When we suffer, or when someone we know is suffering, our prayers are often for healing and restoration. We place our hope in God's mercy and His healing hands. However, we need to be careful when praying this way, because sometimes a full recovery is not what we receive. Sometimes the healing doesn't come. If we only pray this way, we are left questioning God's faithfulness and love for us when our prayers aren't answered the way we want.

What has your understanding been of God's role in suffering and hardship? Circle the words that apply:

Present   Absent   Punishing

Correcting   Guiding

Have you ever experienced blessing within suffering or seen someone receive blessing in their suffering? Like Hagar, were you given a well to provide you with strength to continue on?

In the song Blessings by Laura Story, she asks,

What if your blessings come through raindrops?
What if your healing comes through tears?
What if a thousand sleepless nights are what it takes to know You're near?
What if trials in this life are Your mercies in disguise?

This is not how we are generally told to look at suffering. In fact, most of the time, we are told that suffering is to be avoided at all costs. Aging is something to be avoided with facial creams, Botox, facelifts, and the like. In faith communities, we can be told that suffering is an indication that we are doing something wrong, and we are being punished.

It is a particular grace to be able to see blessings, hope, and joy in the midst of suffering or death. But we will never receive it if we don't ask. We will never see it if we aren't looking. We will never experience God's presence and work in our lives if we don't believe it is possible.

Be Not Afraid

What are Genesis 21:17 and
35:17 telling us?

Be not afraid of suffering.
God is present.
Be not afraid of death.
God will not abandon you.

MY STORY

I had a friend, Melanie, who had terminal breast cancer when I met her. I knew from the day our friendship began that our time together was limited and challenging as she made her way through her routine of chemotherapy, doctor appointments, and deteriorating health.

As part of her illness, she had to deal with a significant amount of pain, since the cancer had spread to her bones. This was one of the worst parts for her. I remember praying for her one day, asking God to please relieve her of this pain. He answered in my heart clearly and loudly, "No." It was enough of a response to startle me out of my prayer for a moment. When I went back in, I was confused. "That was pretty clear, Lord. I'd like to understand more. If you aren't going to take her pain away, are you going to use it for her?" And just as clearly, but in the most gentle and loving voice, my heart filled with, "Yes."

I had to leave that prayer with no more information or insight and wait to see if I had heard correctly. Sure enough, I saw Him work through her pain and heal a part of her that had been broken for so very long.

Her relationship with her mother was a strained one at best. Hurt, pain, and loss filled all the memories and stories of who they were together. On one visit during her illness, Melanie was bathing and asked her mother to wash her back, since it was painful and difficult to reach. Standing at the door, her mother only nodded in the direction of a bath brush and said, "You can use that." With that she left the room. The strain and neglect of their relationship can be accurately summed up in that one interaction.

(continued)

A couple weeks later, one of our mutual friends was with Melanie, helping in her daily activities. Again, there was a bath, and this friend—the most tender of mothers—stepped in and washed Melanie's back gently, lovingly, and with a beautifully healing touch. The love of this mother filled the empty spaces and allowed Melanie to forgive her own mother.

Melanie could finally see that her mother's actions were the only way she knew how to show her love. Even in the bathroom scene, it was not a moment of rejection, but her mother's desperate hope to see that her daughter was still strong enough to care for herself and not actually wasting away in front of her eyes. The emotional damage in their relationship was immediately healed, and they reconciled before she died. Without this suffering and pain, and without the chance for it to be touched and healed, the true healing never would have come to Melanie and her mother. I had heard correctly.

QUESTIONS FOR REFLECTION:

1. *Do you think that God causes suffering, allows suffering, or does some mixture of both?*

2. *Sometimes, it is easier to see the blessings in someone else's sufferings than it is to see in our own. Have you seen someone whose suffering has led them to a better place, or someone who has been comforted within their sufferings?*

3. *Do you have a place in your life that is painful right now? What might God be doing with you through it?*

4. *Can you come to a point of peace with this place, knowing that God is at work? What can you do to be hopeful in this?*

CLOSING PRAYER:

Lord, we don't like to suffer. We know that it can keep us from You, and we can forget that You are closer to us in our suffering than at any other time. Help us, Lord, to see Your blessings in our small sufferings so that we can be ready to look again when they are large and heavy. Remind us that You suffered for us, and in that the greatest blessing was given. Bless us, Lord. *Amen*

Week 3
PERSONAL STUDIES

Be Not Afraid

STRENGTHEN *your* FAITH IN GOD

DAY 1

To anyone who has, more will be given and he will grow rich;
from anyone who has not, even what he has will be taken away.

–Matthew 13:12

There are many ways to train for a marathon. Most methods have you build up from several small runs, to longer runs, and then to a mix of small runs, strengthening workouts, and very long runs. If you have trained well enough and long enough, the marathon is very achievable.

However, the marathon is something that I will never do. I don't know if I could physically endure the training or not, but I am quite sure that I do not have the mental interest to pursue it. I regularly run three miles a couple times a week, and that is all I care to do. If I just jumped into a marathon with only that amount of training, chances are good I would not only be unable to finish, but I would injure myself and be unable to run at all for a while. What little I have would be taken away.

This verse shows us that our faith works in much the same way. If we build up our faith in little ways on a daily basis, then we will be able to rely on it when we need it in times of distress and suffering.

This week, we will focus on what we are doing to build and strengthen our faith. Let's look at our training regimen and see if we need to adjust it a bit.

1. *Indicate which of these practices you do to build your faith regularly (R), periodically (P), occasionally (O), or never (N)*

_____ *Prayer (rote or spontaneous)*

_____ *Reading Scripture*

_____ *Bible study*

_____ *Attend church services*

_____ *Meditation/Contemplation*

_____ *Service to others*

_____ *Confession*

_____ *Journaling*

_____ *Physical expressions of faith*

_____ *Other* _____

2. As we go through life, our physical abilities change. The workout that you loved when you were twenty probably isn't the workout you need when you are fifty. In the same way, our spiritual needs and abilities change at various points in our lives.

   Look back at the list in Question 1 and mark the practices that are working for you right now with a star. (Just because you do them regularly does not mean that they are working or helping.)

   Now, circle any of them that you feel drawn to as a place to grow or change.

   The rest of this week, focus on one starred item and one circled item in the list from Question 1. As you practice them through the week, take note of what they are doing in your life of faith. At the end of the week, we will reflect on the effectiveness of your spiritual workout.

Not only that, but we even boast of our afflictions, knowing that affliction produces endurance, and endurance proven character, and proven character, hope, and hope does not disappoint, because the love of God has been poured out into our hearts through the Holy Spirit that has been given to us.

–Romans 5:3-5

In the last twenty years, the US economy has had several significant downturns. People who never expected to be in difficult financial positions were suddenly losing jobs, homes, savings, and worried about putting food on the table. A friend of mine was affected by one of these downturns, and while she isn't quite ready to boast of her affliction, I can do it for her.

Faced with the uncertainty of unemployment with an economy that was offering little opportunities, it was a time when she didn't know if their savings would get the family through without losing more than just the job.

As her children started back to school, it was hard to justify their tradition of getting a new outfit for the first day. It had always been a fun and exciting part of back to school, but this year, it wasn't going to happen. It was at that point that her heart was touched, and she saw the plight of many who were worse off than she was. With reports of the food pantry running out of food on a regular basis, her eyes were opened to people who wouldn't even eat, much less worry about something like a new outfit for school. An organization was born.

Her life returned to normal, but her heart had been changed. Her organization started as a way to provide clothes and items to those in need without cost, and it quickly grew into an organization focused on breaking the cycle of poverty, while providing for the needs of the families in transition. In a few short years, they have helped thousands of people with items to get them through and skills to get them out.

In her momentary affliction, she had the endurance to bear it, the character to use it for God's purposes, and the hope to know that God could use her to change the world around her. She has not been disappointed.

1. *It can be hard to listen or watch for God's call while in a place of suffering or fear. How can the practices from Day 1 that you are focusing on help you see God more clearly?*

2. *Think of a place of difficulty you are facing now or have faced in the past. What might God being doing with you through it?*

3. *In Romans 5:3-5, Paul lists several effects of afflictions. Which of these do you see in the example you just listed?*

We know that all things work for good for those who love God,
who are called according to his purpose.

– Romans 8:28

This verse is often used as a statement of comfort and purpose in times of pain, but it can be very difficult to hear when you are suffering. Sometimes, what you are going through just doesn't feel good, and it doesn't help to have someone tell you that it should.

It is a particular grace to be able to be joyful or even to focus on the good that can come from something that seems to be very bad. However, we are called to see the blessings in everything that God does in our lives.

> *Consider it all joy, my brothers, when you encounter various trials, for you know that the testing of your faith produces perseverance. And let perseverance be perfect, so that you may be perfect and complete, lacking in nothing.*
>
> –James 1:2-4

Scripture repeatedly tells us to remember that if we love God, and if we are looking for God's will for us, even these points of sorrow and pain can be used for His purpose.

1. *When you have been in a place of suffering, what are some of the things that have brought you strength and comfort?*

2. Have you been able to see the "good" God has brought from your place of suffering?

3. Can the practices that you are focusing on this week help you to accept and believe these words of comfort? How?

4. *For the rest of the week, come back here and reflect on the practices that you are working on from day one. Has there been a difference in your faith life? Are you drawn to continue these practices or move on to something else? How do you see yourself strengthening your faith as you go forward from here?*

Day 4

Day 5

Day 6

Be Not Afraid
OF
FORGIVENESS

Immaculée Ilibagiza survived the Rwandan Holocaust in a tiny bathroom with seven other women. With members of the Hutu tribe hunting and killing people from her own Tutsi tribe, she hid for ninety-one days and withdrew in prayer from the moment she woke up until the moment she went to sleep. She knew that her family members were probably dead, and that some her friends had turned and were now hunting for her. As she prayed the Lord's Prayer, she realized that she did not mean "as we forgive those who trespass against us," and she omitted it from her prayer. There was no way that she could forgive these murderers. After a while, she realized that she couldn't change the words that Jesus told us to pray. Instead, she prayed them, asking God to help her mean them.

It wasn't long before her request was granted. In a vision, she saw Jesus hanging on the cross forgiving the people who had condemned Him and cursed Him. She asked, "How can you forgive them? They are the reason you are on the cross." His answer changed her life. Jesus could forgive them because they were His children, and the evil they were doing was destroying them, not Him. He loved them, and their actions saddened Him. He wanted nothing more than for them to turn away from the evil they were committing. The forgiveness was easy. From that moment on, Immaculée could pray the Lord's Prayer with her whole heart, meaning every word. After the war was over, she was able to confront the person who had killed her mother and brother and forgive him directly. The guilt he carried overwhelmed him, and Immaculée's forgiveness helped to set him free.[1]

Both giving and accepting forgiveness can be difficult. This week we look at a story that shows us the blessings that can come when forgiveness is given and received freely.

THEIR STORY

Joseph and his brothers don't have the best history.[2] Joseph is far down the lineage, but is clearly his father's favorite son. Recall that he is the first son of Rachel, Israel's favorite wife, and first born in the heart of Israel. The brothers get a little tired of the favoritism and go out to the wilderness to kill him. At the last minute, they change their minds and decide to sell him as a slave instead.

Joseph ends up in Egypt, and through a series of fortuitous events, ends up as the first in command next to Pharaoh. Not exactly the brother's plan. In time, a famine has struck the entire land, but because Joseph correctly interpreted Pharaoh's prophetic dream years before, Egypt was prepared and wouldn't suffer the effects of the famine.

However, not far away, Israel's family is starving in Canaan. The brothers are told by their father to travel to Egypt and beg for assistance. Upon their arrival, Joseph recognizes them but keeps his own identity secret.

---

[1] Immaculée Ilibagiza tells her story in her books *Left to Tell*, and *Led By Faith*.

[2] For a fun, and lighthearted way to see this story, check out the musical "Joseph and the Amazing Technicolor Dreamcoat." It is available on DVD, YouTube, or occasionally at a local theater.

They have left Benjamin, the younger son of Rachel, at home with their father. Clearly favoritism remains in Israel's house.

Joseph sends the brothers back to retrieve their brother Benjamin in order to receive assistance. When the brothers arrive home, they find their bags filled with supplies and the money they had offered to Joseph, and they are terrified. They will be thought to be thieves when they go back to Egypt, and chances are pretty good that they will be thrown into prison. They don't realize that Joseph had placed the money in the bags to help them on their journey. On their return, they bring back the money and confess it to the head steward immediately, hoping that he will believe that they had no knowledge of where the money came from. The head steward replies,

> "Be at ease," [Joseph's steward] replied;
> "you have no need to fear. Your God and the God of
> your father must have put treasures in your bags for you.
> As for your money, I received it."
>
> –Genesis 43:23

If you were in the brothers' place, would you have believed the steward's words? Why or why not?

How do you think the brothers responded to this statement?

The steward then takes the brothers and treats them to a kingly welcome, feeding their animals, bathing their feet and preparing them for a dinner with Joseph. At dinner, with all the brothers together, Joseph is ready to test them. He wants desperately to be reunited. But before he can, he needs to know that they regret what they have done. Do they now honor the bond of kinship, even if it is with another favored son?

After a feast, Joseph sends them off again laden with supplies. In doing so, he frames Benjamin for stealing a silver goblet. As Joseph threatens to throw him into jail, the brothers beg for mercy and offer themselves instead. Joseph realizes that they have changed and finally reveals his identity. Not surprisingly, the brothers are stunned.

Can you even imagine what they must have been feeling? Here is the brother that they tried to kill and then sold, now standing before them in a position of such power that he could do anything he wished with them. I know I would have been pretty sure the game was over for all of us.

Joseph, however, has a different perspective. He tells them,

> I am your brother Joseph, whom you once sold into Egypt. But now do not be distressed, and do not reproach yourselves for having sold me here. It was really for the sake of saving lives that God sent me here ahead of you. For two years now the famine has been in the land, and for five more years tillage will yield no harvest. God, therefore, sent me on ahead of you to ensure for you a remnant on the earth and to save your lives in an extraordinary deliverance. So it was not really you but God who had me come here; and he has made of me a father to Pharaoh, lord of all his household, and ruler over the whole land of Egypt.
>
> –Genesis 45:4-8

**Get the
Whole Story:**
Genesis 37,
and 39-47

Not only are they off the hook, but they are actually almost the good guys, just helping God work out His plan. How did that happen? And how had Joseph been able to see it?

In the face of such forgiveness, the brothers are dumbfounded. To top it all off, Joseph is offering them land, food, protection, and reconciliation, asking them to bring their father and settle in Egypt.

> *Take wagons from the land of Egypt for your children and your wives and to transport your father on your way back here. Do not be concerned about your belongings, for the best in the whole land of Egypt shall be yours.*
>
> –Genesis 19:20

The brothers return to Canaan, tell their father the whole story, and set out to return to Egypt with all they have. On the way, Israel offers sacrifices at Beer-sheba. There he receives a vision, with a similar theme as the ones given to his ancestors, consoling him and reminding him of the promise that was made to Abraham at the very beginning: "I will make of you a great nation."

> *"I am God, the God of your father; do not be afraid to go down to Egypt; for I will there make of you a great nation. Not only will I go down to Egypt with you; I will also bring you back here, after Joseph has closed your eyes."*
>
> –Genesis 46:3-4

This is no false forgiveness. This is not forgiveness with a need for revenge. Israel's family joins Joseph in Egypt comforted by the fact that there has been a true reconciliation.

OUR STORY

When someone hurts us, it can be very hard to forgive. The slightest offenses can set relationships at a distance. So, when the offense is something significant, most people understand if we don't forgive. Keeping the focus on what was done to us, however, can make us lose sight of what God is doing with us. No, God does not want us to do evil to each other. Instead, this story shows us that God can take what was meant for harm and turn it to good. In his generous forgiveness, not only could Joseph do what God had for him to do, but he shows that forgiveness can open the door to blessings beyond measure. Finally, in Genesis 46:3-4, Jacob shows us that we don't need to fear accepting the forgiveness that we are given. It is by doing so that more blessing can come.

Be Not Afraid

What are Genesis 43:20 and
46:3-4 telling us?

Be not afraid to forgive.
God is working with you through it.
Be not afraid to reconcile.
God can bless you in it.

Forgiveness is such a difficult topic. It's easy to say, but so much harder to do, especially when you have been offended by someone close to you.

For many years, I did not have the best relationship with one of my family members. Really, it was just downright awful. Most of the time I was angry or hurt by what she had done or said, and I really just wanted to avoid as many interactions as possible.

Now, knowing that this was not the most Christian way to live, I felt bad about the way I felt and reacted to this person, so I took it to confession and asked forgiveness for the unloving ways that I would think about her. This wonderful priest then asked me if I had been praying for her. Oh. Yes. I have. I pray for her a lot, but, probably not in the way that you would like.

Then came my penance, my assignment. I was to pray for God to bless her. A lot. Ummm, not sure I can do that, Father. I'll admit it started slowly, and I only meant it a little bit, but the more I prayed it the more I realized she needed to be blessed beyond measure, and I wanted it for her.

About that time, I had heard someone say that people only hurt you as much as they are hurting. When I looked at my family member, I realized that she was in a great deal of pain emotionally, and the best thing for her and for us was for her to be happy. I had such incredible blessings in my life, and something in her life was amiss. I didn't know what it was or what would make it better, but in short order, I was praying my heart out for her blessing, and I really meant it.

(continued)

Fast forward, and life has changed dramatically. This person's life went through some drastic, but needed changes that improved her life significantly, and our relationship is so much better than I ever dreamed it would be. We can trust each other, challenge each other, confide in each other, and look forward to our time together.

God was definitely at work here, healing our relationship, giving me much more empathy for people struggling in their lives, and bringing healing into her life. Is that what we intended? Absolutely not. I'm just glad that it was what God intended. ❧

QUESTIONS FOR REFLECTION:

1. *If Joseph had taken revenge on his brothers, how would the story have turned out differently for Joseph, the brothers, God's plan, and the future of the Israelites?*

2. *Is there someone in your life that you have found difficult to forgive? What have you done to try to forgive them? What has been the result?*

3. *Have you been in a position where you desire forgiveness? How did it affect you when it was given or refused?*

4. *In the Lord's Prayer, one of the lines asks God to "forgive us our trespasses as we forgive those who trespass against us." If God is going to answer your prayer, does this give you comfort or make you nervous? If it makes you nervous, what do you need to change to make it comfortable?*

CLOSING PRAYER:

Our Father, who art in heaven, Hallowed be Thy name. Thy Kingdom come, Thy will be done, On earth as it is in Heaven. Give us this day, our daily bread. And forgive us our trespasses, As we forgive those who trespass against us. And lead us not into temptation, But deliver us from evil. Amen

Week 4
PERSONAL STUDIES

Be Not Afraid

LEARN
to
TRUST GOD

> *Then Peter approaching asked him,*
> *"Lord, if my brother sins against me, how often*
> *must I forgive him? As many as seven times?"*
> *Jesus answered, "I say to you, not seven times,*
> *but seventy-seven times."*
>
> –Matthew 18:21-22

I bet that this is a lesson you are dreading. I'm pretty sure that you have someone in mind that you need to forgive. Perfect. If you don't, then I'm pretty sure that you will be given a situation this week that will bring you right into this lesson.

Here we go.

1. *Write down the name of the person in your life that you need to forgive:*

2. *List three things that God would love about this person:*

3. *If you were free of the burden of the offenses that need to be forgiven, how would your life be different?*

4. *Most people think that forgiveness means restoring a relationship, but that isn't necessarily so. If you could forgive this person and let go of the hurt, anger, and resentment, what would that future relationship look like?*

I will give you the same assignment I was given. This week, pray for God to bless this person. Pray every day, and if you don't mean it, ask God to help you mean it. Just keep praying. We'll come back at the end of the week and write down how it went.

DAY 2

*Then the devil took him to the holy city, and made him
stand on the parapet of the temple, and said to him,
"If you are the Son of God, throw yourself down. For it is
written: 'He will command his angels concerning you,' and
'with their hands they will support you, lest you dash your foot
against a stone.' Jesus answered him, "Again it is written,
'You shall not put the Lord, your God, to the test.'"*

–Matthew 4:5-7

Have you ever done a high ropes course? My daughter is deathly afraid of heights, and when she first tried to climb a pole to get to a small platform, she got stuck about halfway up the pole. She couldn't go up, and she couldn't go down. The whole time, she was connected to a belay, or safety rope, that would not let her drop more than a couple inches if she let go or fell. There was no way to convince her that she was safe, so she had to come to a point where she could continue on and finish the course on her own or she was never coming down. Fortunately, she made it. She is now safely back on solid ground and all the more confident in her ability to overcome a challenge.

It reminds me that many times, we can't see the very things supporting us that we can trust to catch us when we fall. We can't see the safety rope God has attached to us, and we don't feel like we will be caught if we fall. There is a delicate balance between blind, misplaced trust and faithful trust. Our verse today shows us that even Jesus had to figure that one out.

How did the devil tempt Jesus to doubt His ability to trust in Matthew 4:5-7?

What was Jesus' response?

In order to forgive, we have trust that God knows what is best when He tells us to forgive, to turn the other cheek, and to pray for those who hate us. How do we develop our trust in God? Let's look at ways we develop trust in our everyday lives, and let's see if we can use that to help us figure it out.

1. *Think of a person or organization that you trust. Why do you trust them? How are you different with them than with people or organizations that you don't trust?*

2. *The more we experience someone as trustworthy, the more we can trust him or her. What kinds of experiences or actions help you trust someone?*

3. *What kind of experience have you had with God that helps you to trust in Him?*

4. *St. Jerome says, "Ignorance of scripture is ignorance of Christ." Jesus and the devil both used scripture in Matthew 4:5-7. How might knowledge or ignorance of scripture affect your ability to develop trust in God?*

DAY 3

Read the following prayer attributed to Mother Theresa of Calcutta:

> People are often unreasonable, irrational, and self-centered.
> Forgive them anyway.
>
> If you are kind, people may accuse you of selfish, ulterior motives.
> Be kind anyway.
>
> If you are successful, you will win some unfaithful friends
> and some genuine enemies. Succeed anyway.
>
> If you are honest and sincere, people may deceive you.
> Be honest and sincere anyway.
>
> What you spend years creating, others could destroy overnight.
> Create anyway.
>
> If you find serenity and happiness, some may be jealous.
> Be happy anyway.
>
> The good you do today will often be forgotten.
> Do good anyway.
>
> Give the best you have, and it will never be enough.
> Give your best anyway.
>
> In the final analysis, it is between you and God.
> It was never between you and them anyway.

Circle the sentence that speaks most to you right now.

Each one of these lines lists a reason for us not to forgive. Each of these lines lists a reason for us to stand in fear and refuse to try.

1. What are we told to do in the face of each of these situations? Why?

2. How does the understanding that all of this is between you and God help you to trust that God can work in the places where it is hardest for you to forgive, or where it is hardest for you to accept forgiveness?

3. Look at the line you circled. Can you "do it anyway?" Why or why not?

4. How does this help with your assignment to bless the person you are called to forgive this week?

For the rest of the week, write out your prayer for that person each day. See if you are starting to mean it. As you pray for this person, what has God done in you and through you? Write your thoughts here.

Day 4

Day 5

Day 6

Be Not Afraid
OF
FEAR

In his inaugural address of 1933, Franklin D. Roosevelt said, "The only thing we have to fear is fear itself—nameless, unreasoning, unjustified terror which paralyzes efforts to convert retreat into advance." The country was in the height of the depression, and there was no way to candy-coat it. He didn't even try. Instead, he described the worst obstacle to overcoming this challenge. With our study titled Be Not Afraid, it seems like we need to address the elephant in the room for at least one lesson. What happens when we succumb to our fear? What happens when we let it overtake our efforts? Is there ever a time when fear is useful? Fortunately for us, we have some examples.

THEIR STORY

Most people don't know that the Israelites arrived at the Promised Land only a year after they left Egypt. No wandering, no long desert punishment, just a small detour at Mount Sinai for some commandments then on to the Promised Land. As they approached the land, twelve scouts were sent ahead to assess the situation. Ten came back scared to death saying, "we cannot attack these people; they are too strong for us" (Numbers 13:31). They went to the Israelites spreading terrifying stories and convincing them to abandon the plan to enter the land. Two of the scouts had a different perspective.

"You need not be afraid of the people of that land; they are but food for us! Their defense has left them, but the Lord is with us. Therefore, do not be afraid of them"

–Numbers 14:9

"The Lord, your God, has given this land over to you. Go up and occupy it, as the Lord, the God of your fathers, commands you. Do not fear or lose heart."

–Deuteronomy 1:21

These two scouts, Caleb and Joshua, saw the same things the other ten had seen, but had a very different perspective. They knew that this was the land God had promised, and they believed that God would be with them as they entered it, no matter how intimidating it appeared. They spread a message of courage and faith, reminding the Israelites of the promise and command of God.

Get the Whole Story:
Deuteronomy 1-4
Numbers 13-14

Did the Israelites listen? The people of God walked through the Red Sea, they received the Ten Commandments, but they just couldn't get past the fact that the people occupying the territory they were supposed to settle were really, really big. It didn't matter that their leaders told them not to fear. It didn't matter that their leaders told them that God was with them. They couldn't remember the times God had been faithful and delivered them from impossible situations. They couldn't hear the voices of truth over the voices of their fear, and they refused to enter. The miracles they had seen just weren't enough.

The Israelites were not ready to enter into the Promised Land, so they had to go back into the desert until they could overcome their fear and trust that God would remain true to His promise. It took forty more years.

Have you faced a fearful situation and backed away, even though your fears were unfounded?

What were the blessings or benefits that could have come if you had overcome your fear?

In our next story, we have an example of when fear can be appropriate and helpful.

We go back a little to Mount Sinai, just after Moses has received the Ten Commandments. It was a pretty incredible sight when he was up there on the mountain. The mountain was smoking, and there were thunder, lightning, and trumpet blasts. The Israelites had been told to stay away from the mountain. Not only that, they had to purify themselves for two days just to be in the vicinity of the mountain.

The Israelites didn't need to be reminded. As they watched and heard all the commotion, they began slowly backing away. They asked Moses, "You speak to us, and we will listen; but let not God speak to us or we shall die" (Exodus 20:19). In other words, "You go to the mountain. We'll stay waaaay over here."

> *Moses answered the people, "Do not be afraid,*
> *for God has come to you only to test you and put*
> *his fear upon you, lest you should sin."*
>
> —Exodus 20:20

Get the
Whole Story:
Exodus 19-20

In the next few verses, God speaks through Moses and makes sure that the Israelites are clear about His authority.

> *"You have seen for yourselves that I have spoken to you from heaven. Do not make anything to rank with me; neither gods of silver nor gods of gold shall you make for yourselves."*
>
> –Exodus 20:22-23

The Israelites got a glimpse of the power of God. This is not some little fairy tale, but a powerful and formidable God. God was making it clear to the Israelites that the law they were about to receive was not to be taken lightly.

From there the law is spelled out in great detail for the Israelites. In fact, it fills up the next three chapters of Exodus, (Exodus 21-23) and is followed by chapter after chapter full of details and instructions to build a dwelling place for God in their midst. This is not some fly by night relationship here. This is serious.

OUR STORY

Isn't Moses' response a little funny? "Don't be afraid, because God just wanted to make you afraid of him." That doesn't seem like the type of God most of us want to have. We like the God who loves us, picks us up when we are down, and forgives us no matter what we do. I agree. That is a great God, and it is a true aspect of who He is.

But, at some point, we need to remember that He isn't just some Santa figure who grants all our wishes and gives us whatever we want. He *is* actually God. He *is* bigger than anything we know. He *is* more powerful than we could ever hope to be. He *did* create all things. We didn't. We can't. We need to understand who He really is, and then keep it in balance.

Understanding that God is God helps us know that His view of what is in front of us is better than our own. Understanding that God is God helps us listen when he demands more of us than we think we can handle. Understanding that God is God helps us follow his commands, even when they don't allow us to live as we think we should. Understanding that God is God helps us value those moments when He comes down so gently to pick us up and set us back on our feet. Understanding that God is God helps us stand in awe and gratitude at the forgiveness that is offered to us so freely. Understanding that God is God helps us know that the fear of the Lord is something to be desired, not rejected.

Be Not Afraid

What are Numbers 14:9, Deuteronomy 1:21,
and Exodus 20:20 telling us?

Be not afraid of being afraid.
God can use our fear
to protect us.

MY STORY

I love children. The way they discover the world every day helps me rediscover the wonders of creation. The miracle of a doodlebug rolled up into a ball, coming out of its shell to wander across the ground, then rolling up again as a chubby finger touches it is a delight through the eyes of a fascinated child. I love being part of a child's discovery and try to set up a world around them to help make that happen.

When a neighbor boy was helping me walk a dog—a very small one, mind you—it was with the same spirit of discovery that I allowed him control of the leash. Who knows what you will find when you follow the impulses of a dog?

I saw the two of them wandering up the street with the little boy skipping along behind, even though I had told him to stay in the yard. As they got closer and closer to the entrance road to the neighborhood, I knew I couldn't reach them in time and yelled in the harshest voice I could for him to stop. Immediately. He stopped and came back to me, quite upset. I apologized for frightening him, and he asked me never to yell at him like that again. I couldn't promise him that.

I had frightened the poor boy to death, but I needed him to be afraid. He wouldn't have listened to me otherwise and would have headed straight into danger. I knew he could control the dog. I knew he had the strength. I needed to give him the will to do it in the first place.

QUESTIONS FOR REFLECTION:

1. *Research shows that we tend to give more credibility to negative statements than to positive statements. How does that fact show the power of fear in our perceptions?*

2. *What is something you can do to counter the power of fear in the face of a challenging situation?*

3. *What is your understanding of God? Does it lean more toward God as a wish-granter, an unreasonable rule maker, or somewhere in between?*

4. *How do you think that the fear of the Lord could be a virtue or a good quality to have?*

 **CLOSING PRAYER:**

God, You are God, and we are not. Remind us of whom You are, so that we can remember who we are in Your eyes. We are the Beloved of a mighty God, who knows our weakness, who knows our frailty, and who knows our greatness in You. In You, we can do all things. Without You, we can do nothing. When You test us, help us to fear You in a way that strengthens our faith. Do not let us be fainthearted. Bless us, Lord. *Amen*

Week 5
PERSONAL STUDIES

Be Not Afraid

GROW
in
WISDOM

May the eyes of [your] hearts be enlightened, that you may know what is the hope that belongs to his call, what are the riches of glory in his inheritance among the holy ones, and what is the surpassing greatness of his power for us who believe, in accord with the exercise of his great might.

–Ephesians 1:18-19

Wisdom and knowledge are two different things. You can get straight A's in school and have no idea how to navigate the world around you. You can have the Bible memorized, be able to recite it in the original translation, or even have a degree in theology, but have absolutely no faith.

Wisdom is defined as "the quality of having experience, knowledge, and good judgment." Experience helps us to develop wisdom. It is important to study and gain knowledge, but we must not stop there. The thing that changes us is when our understanding of God leads us into a relationship with God. It is there that we take those points of experience and knowledge and turn them into moments of wisdom and grace. Our verse today shows us some of the qualities of the wisdom we gain as we grow closer and closer to God. It is our hearts that are enlightened, and we begin to understand the hope, riches, and greatness that have been there the entire time. We have been building this in our study as we learn what God has to say in Scripture, and we look closely at our experiences. This week is the time when we start to own it.

Each of these three Bible verses tells us something about our relationship with God. Read each of them and pick the one that speaks to you the most at this moment.

> "Trust in the Lord with all your heart and on your own intelligence rely not; in all your ways be mindful of him, and he will make straight your paths."
>
> –Proverbs 3:5-6

> "The Lord is my light and my salvation; whom do I fear? The Lord is my life's refuge; of whom am I afraid?"
>
> –Psalm 27:1

> "They shall be my people, and I will be their God. One heart and one way I will give them, that they may fear me always, to their own good and that of their children after them."
>
> –Jeremiah 32:38-39

Take the verse that speaks to you the most and write it on a card or piece of paper. You can make it simple, decorate it, print it large, or print it small. Place it somewhere that you will see it every day. At the end of the week, you will come back and write about what God has told you through this verse. We will answer these questions: Has the meaning changed? Has it been relevant in your daily life this week? What has God done with you through it?

But if any of you lacks wisdom, he should ask God who gives to all generously and ungrudgingly, and he will be given it.

–James 1:5

We live in an instant gratification world. We can reach people in seconds, even if they are a continent away. We can watch movies or television series on demand, and two-day deliveries are more the norm than the exception.

So, when we read a verse like James 1:5, we may grow impatient as we wait for the wisdom that is promised. It is easy to see this as a wish-granting verse, and give up on it if we don't feel wise in a matter of days or even weeks.

But, now we know that God's promises don't always happen in the time frame we expect. Abram waited twenty-five years, Joseph was separated from his family for many years, and the Israelites took forty years to get to the Promised Land. We have learned that to grow in wisdom, we must grow in knowledge, experience, and right judgment. We are called to be patient, to be active, and to look for the moments of grace that open our eyes to the wisdom of God.

1. *What point of wisdom has been developing in you during this study?*

2. *What insights have you developed over the last few weeks?*

3. *What would help you increase in knowledge or experience in this area of wisdom?*

4. *Does the verse you are focusing on this week speak to this point of wisdom? What does it say?*

Today, ask God to help you develop wisdom. Ask in faith, knowing that God would love to give you such a gift.

For the rest of the week, we will review the verse from Day 1 that you chose for this week. The verses are:

> *"Trust in the Lord with all your heart and on your own intelligence rely not; in all your ways be mindful of him, and he will make straight your paths."*

–Proverbs 3:5-6

> *"The Lord is my light and my salvation; whom do I fear? The Lord is my life's refuge; of whom am I afraid?"*

–Psalm 27:1

> *"They shall be my people, and I will be their God. One heart and one way I will give them, that they may fear me always, to their own good and that of their children after them."*

–Jeremiah 32:38-39

Each day, write out your verse, and anything from that day that has brought your verse to mind or made your verse relevant.

Day 3

Day 4

Day 5

Day 6

1. *Has the meaning of your verse changed?*

2. *Has it been relevant in your daily life this week?*

3. *What has God done with you through it?*

4. *Write here about anything that has happened with this verse this week.*

Be Not Afraid
OF
LEADERSHIP

George Washington is the only president elected by unanimous vote in the Electoral College. As the leader of the Continental Army, and the one who led the United States to freedom, he seemed the natural choice. The only person who seemed to be unsure of the selection was George Washington himself.

Since this is our last lesson, we will do things a little differently. We will have a brief lesson and take the time to complete the discussion questions, and then we will continue with a review of the study, and a second round of discussion questions.

In *George Washington: A Life*, Ron Chernow details Washington's private letters where he compares his ascending to the presidency to "a culprit who is going to the place of his execution." He responds to the messenger delivering the news of his election by again voicing his doubts in his ability to fulfill the role of president in the manner that the country expects. This is the man who has conquered a world superpower, with territory all across the globe. This is a man who has led an untrained army of volunteers against a regimented, trained army of professional soldiers. How could he be afraid?

In our lesson today, we will look at Moses' and Joshua's calls to lead the people of Israel into the Promised Land. It is not uncommon for leaders to be a bit nervous as they are called to lead.

THEIR STORY

When God called Moses to lead the people of God out of Egypt, he was not interested at first. He argues backand forth, claiming that the Israelites would never believe him, pointing out his inability to speak well, and even insisting, "If you please, Lord, send someone else!" (Exodus 3:13)

In response, God provides proof after proof that leadership is what He requires of Moses, and that Moses will not be left alone in it. Moses is told to throw down a staff, and it turns into a snake. He is told to pick it up, and it returns to being a staff. His hand is covered in leprosy and healed. Finally, his brother Aaron is sent to help Moses and give him the confidence to lead. God comforts Moses, telling him "I will assist both you and him in speaking and will teach the two of you what you are to do." (Exodus 4:15b) Moses is not called to lead because he is qualified. Moses is called to lead because God can work through him.

Many years later, Moses and the Israelites are standing at the edge of the Promised Land, ready to go in. Moses has been admonishing them, and preparing them to enter. He has given them their history, laid out the plan for their future, and given them guidance on the way they are to live to remain in communion with their God. Moses finishes by telling them that he will not be going with them into the Promised Land. God will be with them, and Joshua will be their guide. All that is left to do is transfer power.

> *Then Moses summoned Joshua and in the presence of all Israel said to him, "Be brave and steadfast, for you must bring this people into the land which the Lord swore to their fathers he would give them; you must put them in possession of their heritage. It is the Lord who marches before you; he will be with you and will never fail you or forsake you. So do not fear or be dismayed."*
>
> –Deuteronomy 31:7-8

Moses knows that leading the people into the Promised Land is a difficult role. He reminds Joshua that God is clearing the way. Joshua has been called to lead, and God will be with him as he does. He does not need to be afraid.

Get the Whole Story:
Deuteronomy
31:1-14

OUR STORY

Some people are natural leaders. They pick up the mantle at every organizational meeting, they start their own businesses, and they run for public office with seemingly little trepidation. But even they have moments where leadership can be a challenging task. On September 11, 2001, President George W. Bush was faced with a presidency that was going to be very different from the one he had been anticipating. The new CEO of a struggling company has the daunting task of turning the business around.

Most of us, though, will not be in leadership roles of such magnitude. We are called to lead in small ways and in ways that we may not even consider leadership. Sometimes we are called to lead in a way that we don't think we're capable. Each time, we have to listen to the voice of God in our hearts and see if we are being given proof that we can do it with God's help.

In Deuteronomy 31:7-8, Moses shows us another type of leadership that all of us must participate in. Just as Joshua was called to bring the people of Israel into the Promised Land, we are called to be witnesses of God and lead people to Him. We may not feel ready, we may not feel equipped, but we can be sure that the promise God made to Moses and Joshua is the same promise that we are given. In fact, Jesus tells us so:

> Then Jesus approached and said to them, "All power in heaven and on earth has been given to me. Go therefore, and make disciples of all nations, baptizing them in the name of the Father, and of the Son, and of the holy Spirit, teaching them to observe all that I have commanded you. And behold, I am with you always, until the end of the age."
>
> –Matthew 28:18-20

This command and promise are not only for the apostles, but for all of us. Usually, when we read this, we think about missionaries in Africa or some other exotic location. While there are people who are called to do mission work in distant lands, most of us are called to work right where we live. It can be in our workplaces, in our schools, and even in our own homes. No matter where it is, we are promised that God will be with us as we lead others to Him.

St. Theresa of Avila summarizes our role beautifully:

Christ has no body now but yours. No hands, no feet on earth but yours.
Yours are the eyes through which he looks with compassion on this world.
Yours are the feet with which he walks to do good.
Yours are the hands through which he blesses all the world.
Yours are the hands, yours are the feet, yours are the eyes, you are his body.
Christ has no body now on earth but yours.

Give an example of how we can be a part of each of the categories listed in
St. Theresa of Avila's quote:

Eyes:

Feet:

Hands:

If we have been given the gift of faith, even one as small as a mustard seed, we are called to remember:

You are the light of the world. A city set on a mountain cannot be hidden.
Nor do they light a lamp and then put it under a bushel basket; it is set
on a lampstand, where it gives light to all in the house. Just so, your light
must shine before others, that they may see your good deeds, and glorify
your heavenly Father.

–Matthew 5:14-16

All of us are called to share our light with others. Keeping our faith to ourselves has never been an option we could choose.

Be Not Afraid

What is Deuteronomy 31:7-8 telling us?

Be not afraid of leading others to God.
God will march before you.

MY STORY

A few years ago, I was given an opportunity to lead a group of high-school students in a faith formation class. This was going to be a different format than any other class I had done before, but it was a format that I really felt called to lead. It was going to be more of a dialogue class and I would welcome the hard questions, the struggles, and the doubts. We were going to wrestle. I looked at these just-barely-teens and saw how easily they dismissed adults and teachers as irrelevant and unimportant. I saw the rolling eyes in church as their parents made them attend. I was supposed to lead these kids to faith? Oh, yes, I was.

I stepped out, still a bit afraid. I only invited five kids that I already knew well to join my group. Then word got out and other parents asked if their children could join the group. The kids attending asked if they could invite friends. My small, safe, intimate group quickly grew to twenty plus, and they all came each week for three years. After that, schedules became too busy and too varied for us to meet on a regular basis, so we agreed to a small text when I had something I wanted them to know or learn. That small text has continued to this day and is how my blog was started. God had more people for me to lead.

(continued)

In the end, I didn't know all the answers, and we struggled with some of them together for quite a while. But, as intimidating as it seemed, there was really nothing to be afraid of. These teens were hungry for someone to acknowledge their questions and for a place to ask them without fear of judgment. I learned so much from them as I had to look for the answers they wanted. I was given such joy when I would hear them process their questions and realize that they often had the answer the whole time.

God called me to lead, and to lead without fear. He didn't mind my trepidation. He just blew right through it. All it took was for me to step forward in it.

QUESTIONS FOR REFLECTION:

1. *What are some ways that you have been able to share your faith with others since you have started this study?*

2. *How do you think God is calling you to use your talents or your personality to reach out to others?*

3. *How do you think God is asking you to challenge yourself in sharing your faith with others?*

4. *How can you place your trust in God's plan for your leadership? Does that change what you are doing? How or why?*

CONCLUSION

We have walked through many aspects of fear and their antidotes. We have seen how God is faithful, how God will challenge us, how God will make us uncomfortable, how God will comfort us, how God will bless us, and many more.

As we complete our study, let us review each lesson and see how we have grown in our faith, trust, and understanding of God. Let us rediscover how we are called to overcome our fears, and live a life of faith. Take a few minutes to look over each summary, and answer the questions. Don't worry if you can't answer all of them. God will have something to tell you in the ones you are able to answer. When you are done, discuss your answers as a group.

Lesson 1: Delays

Abram waits and waits for an heir, Isaac is moved time and time again until he reaches the land where he can settle. Through them, God tells us not to be afraid when our plans are delayed or re-routed. We are to rest in faith, listening for the small, quiet whisper that can come amid storms and fire.

Have you found that you have been able to wait in faith since this study started? Do you have a specific example?

Lesson 2: Obstacles

The Israelites face trial after trial as they work their way to the Promised Land. From armies trapping them at the Red Sea, to kings meeting them for battle. Through them, God tells us not to be afraid when we face obstacles in our lives. We are to remember the times that God has been faithful and rest knowing that He will be faithful again.

How have you found that you have been able to remember God's faithfulness since this study started? Do you have a specific example?

Lesson 3: Suffering

Hagar is kicked out of Abraham's camp and is saved just as she reaches the point of death. Rachel dies in childbirth but is allowed to see that she has given birth to a son. Through them, God tells us not to be afraid when we suffer and not to be afraid of death. We are to have hope, knowing that even in suffering, God is present and at work. We are to remember that death is not the end, but a transition to heaven. We are to remember that sorrow does not show lack of faith, but strength of love.

How have you been able to find hope in the midst of suffering or death since this study started? Do you have a specific example?

Lesson 4: Forgiveness

Joseph and Jacob both travel to Egypt. Joseph goes unwillingly as a slave, having been sold by his brothers. Jacob goes in joy, anticipating a reunion with a son who was dead, and abundance for his family in the midst of famine after Joseph has forgiven his brothers. Through them, God tells us not to be afraid to forgive and to reconcile. We are to trust that God can work through the times we have been hurt, and even give us the strength to wish blessing on those who have hurt us.

How have you been able to forgive since this study started? Do you have a specific example?

Lesson 5: Fear

Moses tells the Israelites that God wants them to be afraid of Him, and as they come to the Promised Land, they refuse to enter because their fear takes away their trust in God's promise. In this, God tells us that there are things that we should fear, and warns us of letting our fear cloud our judgment. In fact, fear of the Lord is not something to be afraid of, but something to strive for. We are to grow in wisdom and the ability to discern what we should fear, and what we should dismiss.

How have you been able to discern what is to be feared and what is not to be feared since this study started? Do you have a specific example?

Lesson 6: Leadership

Moses commissions Joshua to lead the people of God into the Promised Land and to remember that God is with them. Through him, God tells us not to be afraid when we are called to lead. We are to step into our leadership role in faith and confidence, knowing that God will continue to guide our steps.

How do you feel you are called to lead after reading this lesson? Do you have a specific example?

CLOSING PRAYER:

Lord, you are faithful. Lord, you are true. You call us to lead, you call us to follow. You call us to trust and you call us to hope. You give us courage, and you give us joy. We have come to you with fears and doubts, and you have answered with love. We thank you for the blessings you have poured on us in this time we have spent with you. Help us to be unafraid. Help us to live in faith in the midst of a fearful world. Bless us, Lord. *Amen*

"My Lord God, I have no idea where I am going.
I do not see the road ahead of me. I cannot know
for certain where it will end. Nor do I really know
myself, and the fact that I think that I am following
your will does not mean that I am actually
doing so. But I believe that the desire to please
you does in fact please you. And I hope I have
that desire in all that I am doing. I hope that I will
never do anything apart from that desire. And
I know that if I do this you will lead me by the
right road, though I may know nothing about it.
Therefore, I will trust you always, though I may
seem to be lost and in the shadow of death. I will
not fear, for you are ever with me, and you will
never leave me to face my perils alone."

- Thomas Merton